Living & Working in Wigan

Listing Wigan Photographers 1850-1925

John Hannavy and Chris Ryan

Smiths Books

Companions to this volume

Maypole: Diary of a Mining Disaster
John Hannavy & Roy Lewis
Pictures of Wigan: 1860-1920
John Hannavy
Wigan Pier: An Illustrated History
John Hannavy & Jack Winstanley
In preparation:
Working in Wigan Mills
John Hannavy & Mairi Macleod
Pictures of Wigan 1920-1960
John Hannavy & Jack Winstanley

Series Editor John Hannavy

cover illustration: Pit Brow Lasses, Wigan Junction Colliery c.1905 (John Hannavy Picture Collection).

Published by Smiths Books (Wigan) Ltd
41-45 Mesnes Street, Wigan. tel. 42810/46270

text © 1986 John Hannavy & Chris Ryan

Designed by Peter J Kneebone MSIAD

ISBN 0 9510680 16

printed by The Hallgate Press, Wigan.

Contents

Acknowledgements 4

Introduction 5

Life & Work in Wigan 7

Wigan Pit Brow Lasses 41

Professional Photography in Wigan 55

List of Wigan Photographers 60

Acknowledgements

The authors and publisher acknowledge with gratitude the part played by many local people and institutions in making this project possible.

Pictures have come from the following sources -
Mrs. G. Armstrong, Mrs. H. Aldred, John Hannavy Picture Collection, The Heyes Family, Lancashire Publications Ltd., Marks & Spencer plc., William Millard, Miss Jean Noble, Alan Robinson, Ernest Savage, Mrs. May Schofield, Trinity College Library Cambridge, Wigan Record Office at Leigh and the Wigan Pier Heritage Centre.

Special thanks are due to the Master and Fellows of Trinity College Cambridge for making the Arthur Munby collection available to us, and to the Librarian and Deputy Librarian and staff for their help with the project. At Lancashire Publications, thanks are due to Bill Anderton, the Editor of the Wigan Observer and to Alan Rimmer, features Editor for their help. Maurice Webster supplied a great deal of information on the Webster family businesses.

Thanks also to Alastair Gillies and Len Hudson at the Borough Archives, and Ted Brownlow at Wigan College of Technology for their help in preparing many of the illustrations for publication.

We must also record our indebtedness to the generations of Wigan photographers without whose talents and endeavours, none of these books would be possible.

Thanks are also due, of course, to our wives who have put up with the domestic upheaval which always runs parallel to an obsession and to Trevor Smith for his confidence in the project.

There are more picture books of Wigan's history in the pipeline. If you have enjoyed this one and feel able to lend your personal mementos of the town's past, you would be helping us immensely. Any material loaned would be copied and returned immediately.

John Hannavy   October 1986

Introduction

This collaboration came about as a result of a chance telephone call - when Chris Ryan and I found that we were working on projects which, if not identical, certainly had numerous features in common. The decision to pool our researches and combine them in a single book was logical.

We have both been fascinated for some time with the essential character of the working Wiganer - a fascination that others have shared before us as this book shows.

Not only was there a considerable breath of employment opportunity in and around Wigan, but there was enthusiasm for work of all sorts evident in the pride with which those workers were prepared to pose for the camera.

This book, therefore, serves three functions. Firstly, as the title suggests, it is about the breath and variety of work undertaken by Wiganers between 1850 and the early 1920s.

Secondly it is concerned with the fascination with Wigan working women in particular experienced by the Victorian eccentric and self-styled anthropolgist, Arthur Munby - whose records of pit girls, mill girls and servants were lavishly illustrated by specially commissioned photography from the town's leading professional photographic studios.

Thirdly, it sets out to list those studios, with the dates during which they were operational, and to provide the armchair historian with a basic guide to dating photographs taken by Wigan photographers which may have found their way into treasured family albums.

Family historians should find their task simplified somewhat by having date parameters within which to investigate further the subject of a Victorian or Edwardian portrait.

1. Steam Tram taking on water, Market Place 1890s. The tractor unit is a Kitson locomotive built at the Airedale Foundry in Leeds between 1893 and 1896. As all steam engines need water, the early Wigan tramway network would have had several hydrant points along the way where the thirsty locomotives could have their tanks replenished. This tram ran on the Wigan-Newtown-Pemberton run.

Life & Work in Wigan

Wigan's history in the second half of the nineteenth century and the first few decades of the twentieth century was domininated by the twin great employers - the mills and the mines. The photographic coverage of Wigan's great past is equally heavily weighted towards those two areas of employment. The well known series of Will Smith's postcard views of the mill girls at Rylands Mill has appeared in many many books ('Pictures of Wigan 1860-1920' being one of the many).

Pit brow lasses appear in so many postcards and photographs that many collectors, I am sure, feel that the girls must have spent more time posing for the cameras of a hundred professional photographers than they spent actually screening coal!

Wigan had three, not two, great industries, however and the third, engineering, is often overshadowed by the image of the town as either a mining town, or a mill town or both.

With several large foundries, forges and engineering plants in the town, there ought to be more interesting photography from that part of Wigan's past than have actually come to light in any of the several picture compilations that have been published over the years.

William Park & Co. had several operations in the town - the well known forge at Ince, and a warehouse in the centre of town in the Wiend. But by far the largest engineering operation was Wigan Coal & Iron Company's huge site at Top Place between Top Lock and Higher Ince. In this second collection of photographs of life and work in Wigan we are publishing-we believe for the first time-two quite remarkable pictures of the interior of that plant taken towards the end of the last century.

At a time when Wigan is changing out of all recognition, when many of the traditional industries have vanished, these poignant reminders of Wigan's past seem more than sixty to a hundred years old. There is so little in them that can be recognised in the Wigan of today that, even for lifelong Wiganers, captions are often needed to place them in today's town.

As with the earlier book 'Pictures of Wigan', there are no empty street scenes in this collection - for Wigan is not and never has been about streets and buildings, it is about people, and it is previous generations of Wiganers who make the town's history a lively subject to study. It was the people whose faces smile or stare out of the pictures which follow who made Wigan the town that it was; a town of mixed industry with a reputation for quality and hard work.

Kirkless Iron and Steel Works has gone; the pits have all gone - and almost all the spoil heaps which kept their locations in the forefront of everyone's consciousness; many of the mill buildings have gone or have been renovated and put to other non manufacturing uses. Most of the pubs on the pages which follow have also gone. Certainly all the shops have disappeared - with the exception of Marks & Spencer, of course.

Only a few tell-tale hints remain to place these pictures firmly on the streets of Wigan between 1860 and 1925.

2. Driver, Conductor and Inspector with electric tram No.45 at Abbey Lakes. This is believed to have been a final inspection run before the regular electric tram service was introduced with these Hurst Nelson tramcars in 1904.

3. Websters Removals. Posing in front of this Foden Excelsior - one of first two in Wigan - is the Webster workforce. William Webster was a miner - saving 2/6 a week from his wages until he could afford a horse and cart from which to sell coal. He then got two more horses and carts for his brothers who were also then working down the mine. When the family moved into haulage, John and Joe were sent to Sandbach to learn to handle the steam lorries. From the right, the people in the picture are John Webster, then Joe Webster, Bill Webster, Tommy King and Billy Jolly. The two on the extreme left are not named. The vehicles could travel at 6 miles per hour on solid metal tyres and, empty, weighed just under five tons. Each morning it took an hour to get up steam - the bags of the cab roof contain the sticks to get the fire going! The family business was based in Darlington Street East. Later William Webster and Alfred Wood owned Middleton & Wood and the Websters also had a coach business, now part of the Smiths Group.

4. Bargee, Leeds Liverpool Canal. For many people, life was lived from one year end to the next on the boats which plied the length of the canal. This picture, probably taken by Rev. Wm. Wickham dates from c1880.

5. "Achilles", was built in 1880 and this picture was taken about the turn of the century. The locomotive was built by Hudswell Clarke in Leeds and worked coal trains from the Standish coalfield at least until the mid 1930s. The locomotive was based at the John Pit sheds in Standish.

6. Locomotive "Lindsay". This locomotive was built at the Wigan Coal & Iron Company's plant at Top Place in 1887 and spent its working life at the Gidlow Washery. Now beautifully restored and painted in a sparkling red livery it can be seen preserved in working order at Steamtown in Carnforth. It was one of several locomotives built to a similar design for use in Wigan collieries.

7. This photograph of a railway accident at Wigan is marked "L&NWR 1904" on the reverse -yet as far as researches can ascertain, there was no railway accident in Wigan in 1904, and the locomotive is a Lancashire & Yorkshire Railway design. Add to that the fact that the bridge is most certainly not one of the L&NWR bridges within the Wigan area, and the picture becomes a bit of an enigma!

6

7

8. A group of fitters pose in front of one of the colliery locomotives at Pemberton Colliery in 1924.

9. The workshop floor in one of the many buildings which made up Wigan Coal & Iron Company's plant at Top Place. The date is probably the 1890s.

9

10

14

10. Also Top Place, at the same time, showing some enormous castings in varying stages of completion. The large block of steel in the middle distance of the picture is stamped "36 tons"! Many of the finished pieces of work in the picture look as though they are destined for a very large ship's engine.

11. The workforce of the Grove Chemical Company in Appley Bridge - the Glue Works which used to be sited at the foot of Appley Lane North. The photograph bears the legend "Presented by the Directors of Grove Chemical Co. Ltd. to Sarah Hatton. Taken in the 21st year of their establishment at Appley Bridge, August 24th 1909".

12. The workforce of Bentley & Jubb posed for this picture in Mesnes Park during the First World War. The company made ammunition, and some examples of their products are lined up in front of the four small boys at the front of the group.

13. Wigan Mill Girls. The two girls in the picture were spinners at one of Wigan's many cotton mills. The girl on the right has on her head the type or hamper/box found in many local mills.

14. These two mills girls are both holding traditional bobbins in their hands. Unfortunately history does not relate which of the town's many mills they worked for.

15. Fletcher's Paperhangings Warehouse was in Millgate, at No.35, a site now cleared and grassed between the new Library and the Radio Manchester studio. Next door to the shop was the local branch of the Miner's Federation. The picture was taken about 1910.

15

L. FLETCHER,
PAPERHANGINGS
WAREHOUSE.
VARNISH,
PAINTS,
BRUSHES,
CUTLERY,
COLLIERY
OILS &c.
SHOW RO
OILS PAI
COLORS
& VARNISHE'S
WAREHOUSE

16. Wilson & Harwood at 28 Market Street were clothiers, pawnbrokers, jewellers and "working man's providers" according to their own advertising. They occupied premises on the site now occupied by the Thomas Cook travel agency.

17. Two policemen, a constable and a sergeant, pose outside a cobbler and leather dealer in Market Place. To the right of the shop is the entrance to the old Fleece Hotel. The site is now occupied by a Building Society and a jeweller.

18. What a difference a few years can make to a location. Today most people remember the corner of Wigan Lane and Coppull Lane as the site of the sadly missed Saracens Head pub, demolished last year to make way for the new ring road. But when John Cooper produced his extensive series of views of Wigan at the turn of the century, that site was occupied by Farrington's boot repair shop. Farringtons later moved along the lane to a more modern shop opposite Lord Street which has also long since been demolished.

19. Peacock's Penny Bazaar, Wigan Market, about 1910. In the earlier days of the Market Hall, butchers, fishmongers and vegetable stalls all operated in amongst the general goods stalls. Here the wide range of goods offered for sale be Peacocks are sandwiched in between sides of beef - a butchers stall is visible on either side of them.

20. Merry Christmas from Wallgate, about 1912. The Yorkshire Bank building is still a shop in this photograph. For this special Christmas version of a Wigan postcard, gold glitter has been glued in lines to look as though it has been strung from the lamp posts as festive decoration.

21. The White Lion Hotel in Hallgate, long since demolished. The photograph was probably taken about late 1880s or early 1890s.

22. Also in Hallgate, and also demolished decades ago, the old Coach & Horses was one of the oldest coaching inns in the town. The buildings dated back at least to the sixteenth century - a bit of genuine half-timbering rather than the Victorian reconstructions which are such a feature of Wigan today.

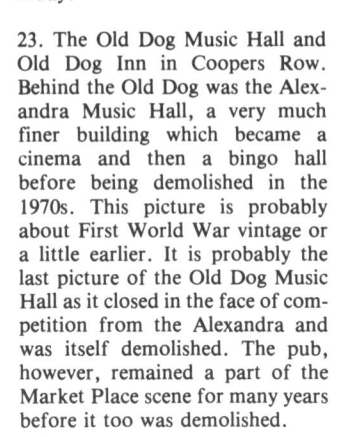

23. The Old Dog Music Hall and Old Dog Inn in Coopers Row. Behind the Old Dog was the Alexandra Music Hall, a very much finer building which became a cinema and then a bingo hall before being demolished in the 1970s. This picture is probably about First World War vintage or a little earlier. It is probably the last picture of the Old Dog Music Hall as it closed in the face of competition from the Alexandra and was itself demolished. The pub, however, remained a part of the Market Place scene for many years before it too was demolished.

24. Royal Albert Edward Infirmary Waiting Room 1920. This, believe it or not, was one of the many postcards you could buy in Wigan - presumably to help pass the time in the waiting room!

23

25

26

24

27

25. Convent schoolgirls waiting to greet the King. Cyril Foley took this delightful picture in Standishgate outside the now demolished convent High School in 1913. The picture was published as part of Will Smith's series of postcards in that same year.

26. It is often forgotten just how close industry and nature were in the Wigan of a hunderd years ago. This picture shows the unusual mixture of farming and heavy industry - in this case paper making - which was a part of the Standish scene a century ago. Taken by John Cooper in the late 1880s, it shows the paper mills on Chorley Road - better known as the bleachworks - behind a traditional farming scene. A reaper drawn by two shire horses is being followed by a team of five farm hands - four women and a boy making the sheafs and stacking them to dry.

27. One man's work is another man's leisure. A light horse and handler with a pleasure craft being towed on the Leeds Liverpool canal near Gathurst at the turn of the century. The picture was taken by amateur photographer J. Hulme Aldred.

28. Wigan's firemen about 1914 with their new Merryweather fire engine.

29. Fire Engine Rally, Market Square. The date is 1890 and the event was the 15th Annual Meeting of the Lancashire Fire Brigades Friendly Society. Wigan's fire engines at the time were the two horse drawn ones in the foreground.

29

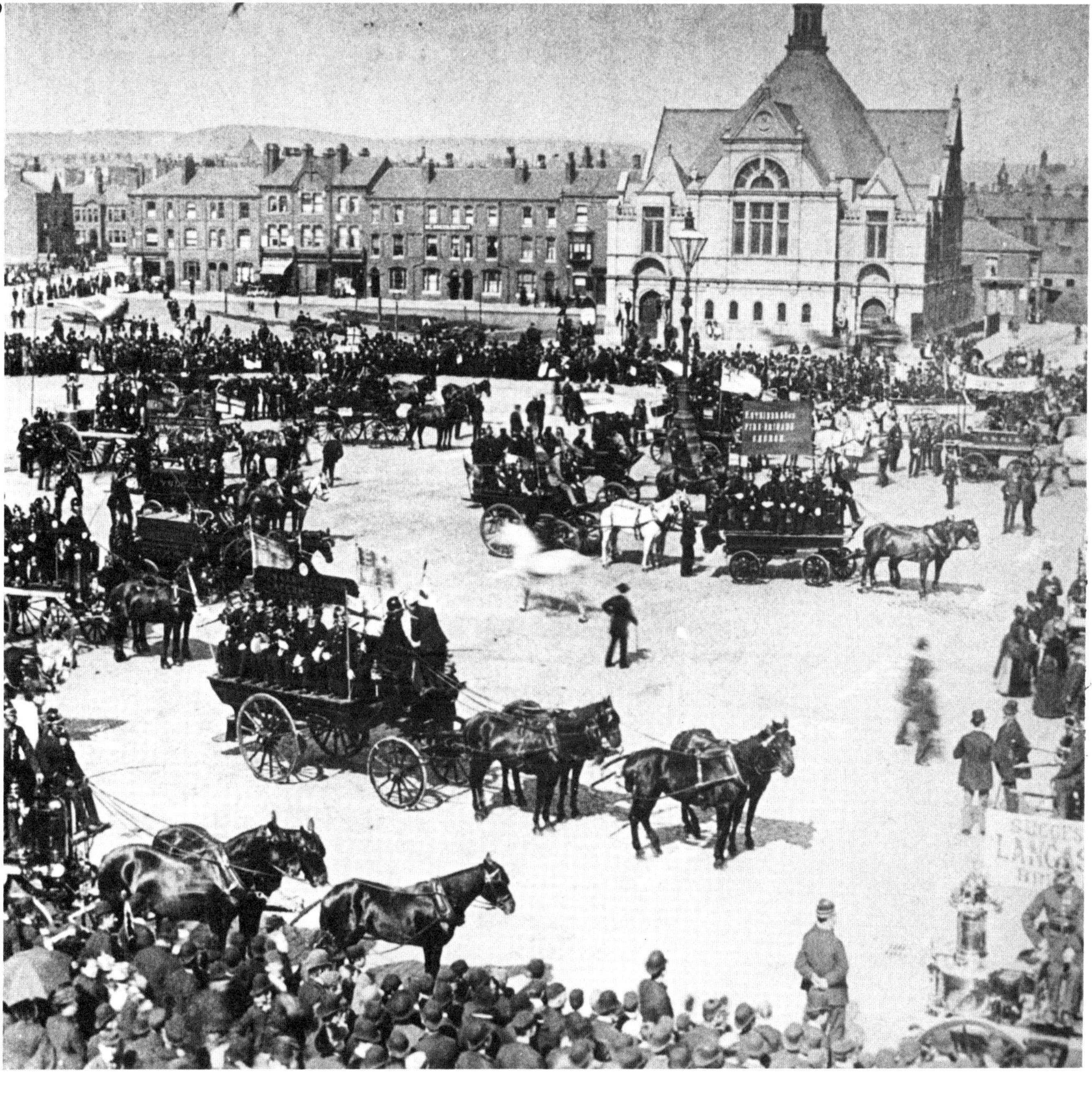

30

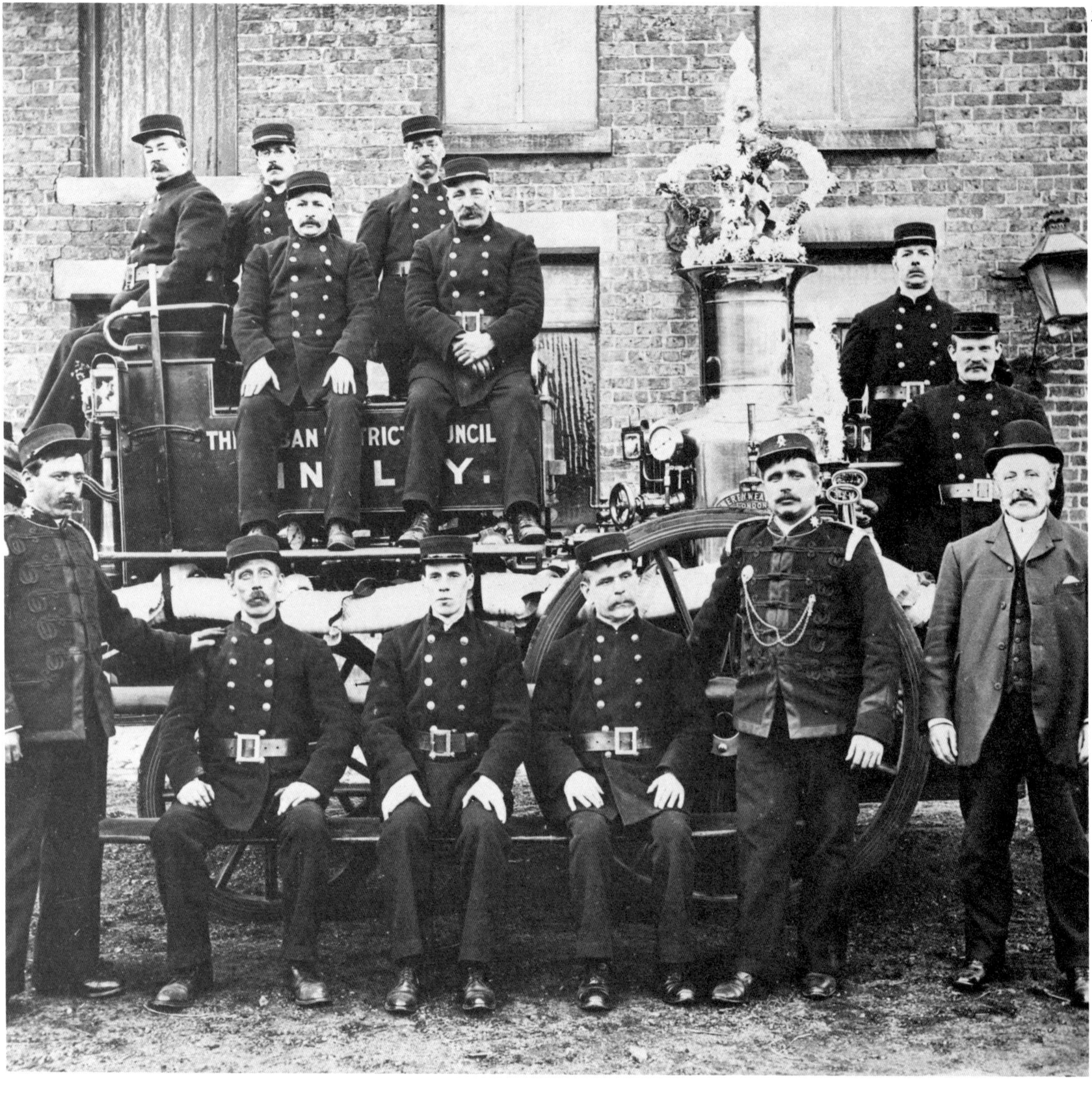

30. Hindley Fire Brigade about the same period. The engine is a horse-drawn Merryweather unit.

31. The premises of J. Holcroft, Iron, Zinc and Tinplate worker were housed under the old library and reading room at Hindley. This picture was probably taken about 1872, some twenty years after the building was opened.

32. Marks & Spencer's Penny Bazaar, Makinson Arcade 1925. Marks had opened a bazaar on Wigan Market some time around 1891 and for a time lived in Wigan. The Makinson Arcade shop was maintained until 1931 when the company built the present Standishgate premises.

33

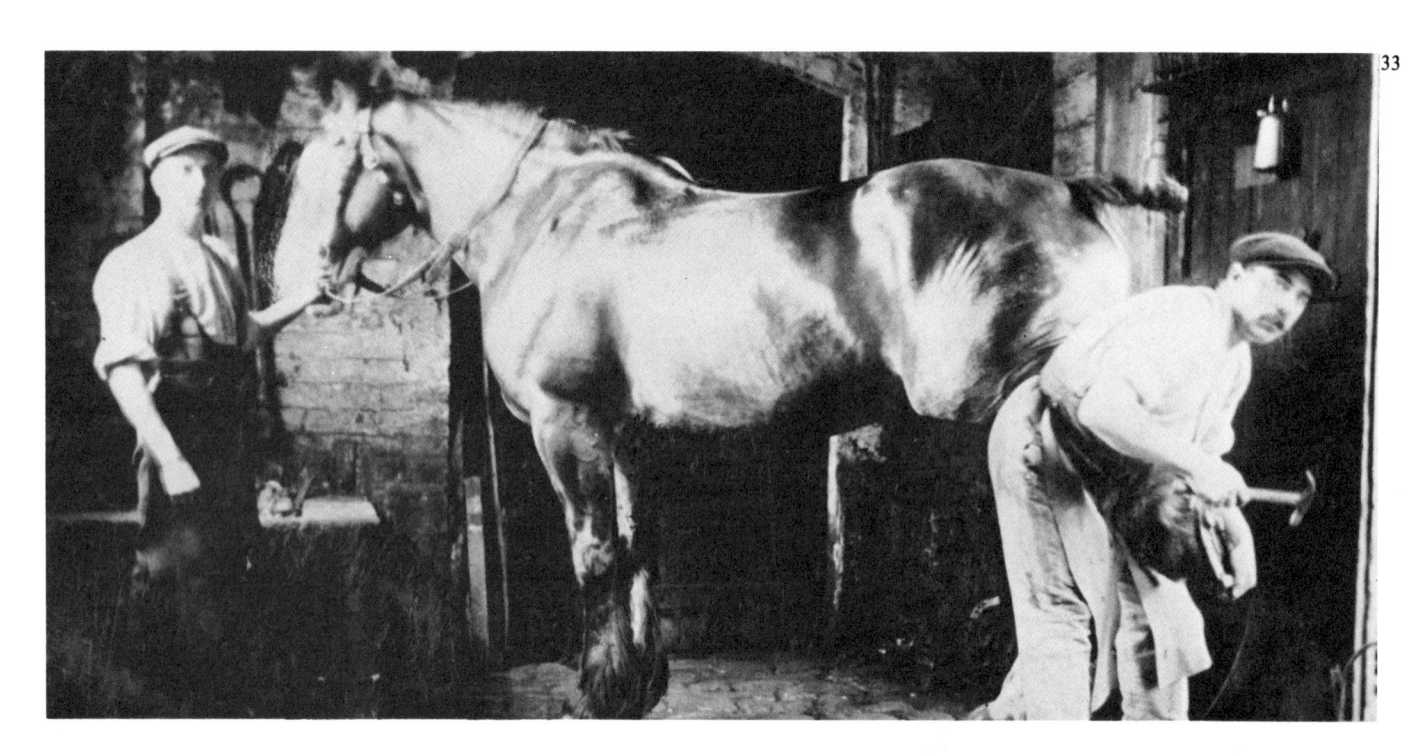

34

33. & 34. Farriers, Wigan Coal & Iron Company, Top Place. The date is about 1918 and the man on the right was Ted Santus. He later left Top Place to set up his own blacksmith's business in the town.

35. William Parks & Company's warehouse in the Wiend at the turn of the century. The company manufactured a wide range of metal products from small hand tools to very much larger pieces of equipment. The warehouse held their iron and steel stock-holdings and were only moved to the Ince site in 1950.

36

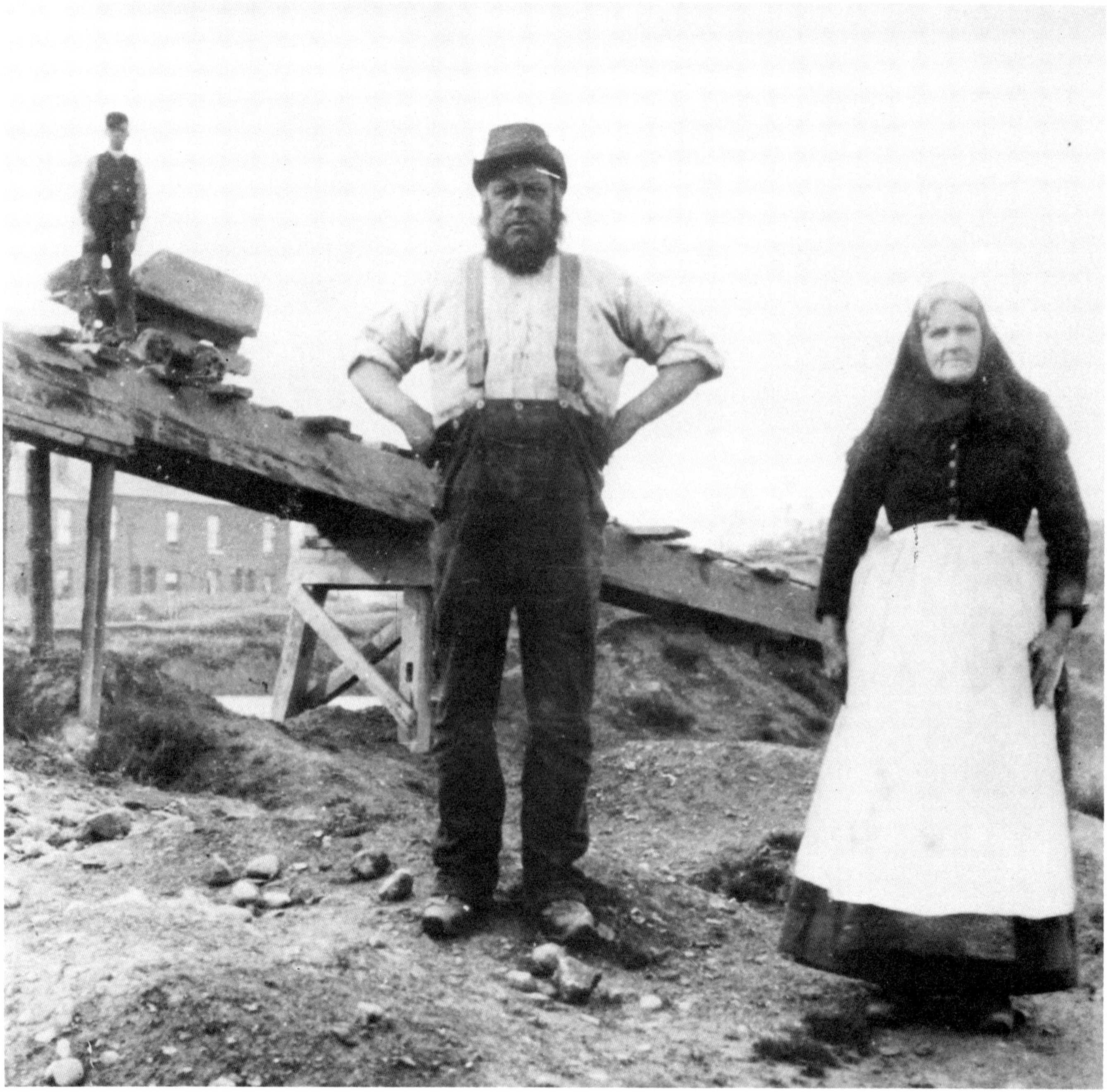

36. Brick Makers, 1891 - one of a remarkable series of pictures taken by Wigan amateur photographer, the Rev. William Wickham.

37. Ponies and their handlers at Pemberton Colliery c.1905. In the background can be seen three of the four sets of winding gear which Pemberton had at its peak of production. The ponies were being broken in on the surface before starting work underground.

38. Shevington Basket Pit c.1836. This photograph is part of the collection assembled by Arthur Munby whose fascination with the lives and working conditions of Wigan's Pit lasses is chronicled in the next chapter of this book.

39. The men from the Maypole Rescue Team preparing to go down the Pretoria Pit at Westhoughton after the disaster there in 1910. Many of the lessons learned during the ill-fated Maypole explosion - where rescue teams used breathing equipment for the first time - were standard procedure by the time of the Pretoria disaster. Three hundred and forty four men died in that disaster, over four times as many as had died at Wigan's Maypole Disaster two years previously.

40. Winstanley Basket Pit 1880. The baskets were used both to haul coal up to the surface and to transport men - three at a time - down the shaft.

41. Pit Lass. A studio portrait by Herbert Wragg of 45 Mesnes Street, Wigan taken about 1886. The girl probably worked for Lamb & Moores at one of their local collieries as Wragg produced several studies of girls working for that company.

40

41

WRAGG
WIGAN

42

42. An eleven ton block of cannell coal cut from Junction Colliery in 1880. Cannell coal burned with an intense heat and very little waste. It found many uses. Much of the cannell cut from Wigan collieries was used in the manufacture of coal gas to light the streets and houses of Wigan. It was also such fine texture that it could be carved, and legend has it that the Earl of Crawford and his guests on one occasion ate a meal off cannell plates - and then stoked the fire with them afterwards - which is one way to cut down on the washing up! Twenty years later, a further generation of pit brow lasses from Junction colliery posed for the picture used on the cover of this book.

43. Pit Brow Lasses, Bamfurlong Colliery c.1905, photographed by Thomas Taylor of Platt Bridge.

44. Interior of Bamford's Mountain Bakery, Wright Street, Whelley in 1905. Low lighting levels inside the bakery meant long exposure times so this is a very posed picture - with the five lads all resting their arms on something sturdy to keep them from moving.

45. & 46. Haigh Brewery about the turn of the century. In the first photograph nine drays complete with horses and handlers are drawn up in front of the building. The Balcarres Arms is at the left hand side. In the second photograph, inside the brewery yard, twenty members of the workforce - predominantly women except for six men who are presumably coopers and their apprentices - lined up for the camera.

47. McDermot's fruit and vegetable stall, Wigan market Hall 1877. This picture was taken the year the Market Hall was opened and long before many of the produce stalls were banished either to the open market outside or to ill-advised extensions to the original building. The most likely location for this stall is the corner of Market Street and the Market Square.

48. Bluecoat Schoolroom c1905. On the wall between the windows is the Golden Jubilee picture of Queen Victoria who had been dead only a few years, while to the right of the teacher, the Coronation portrait of the new King and Queen hangs just underneath a gas lamp -the brightest position on the wall. The picture was probably taken by one of the Millard family of professional photographers.

49

50

Wigan Pit Brow Lasses

Between the 1850s and 1880s Wigan's Pit Brow Girls found themselves the centre of an obsessive and unusual study by Arthur Joseph Munby (1828-1910), a middle class Victorian gentleman, trained barrister, poet and amateur artist. He was a respected figure in the literary and social circles of London and working as a clerk for the Ecclesiastical Commission - a job that he did not consider particularly fulfilling, he found sufficient time to follow his own personal interests. Munby's all-consuming obsession was in meeting and recording in his diaries the details of the everyday lives of working women. He spoke to Yorkshire fisherwomen, London milkwomen, household servants and Black Country brickworkers. He was fascinated by the sort of work considered by genteel society to be unsuitable for women, and of all these women he met in his travels his favourites were Wigan's pit brow girls.

It is difficult to unravel how and why Munby became so interested in the minute details of the lives of working women. Like many members of Victorian society, his interest may have been aroused by the findings of the Children's Employment Commission in 1842. The Commission was set up to investigate the conditions under which children worked in mines. In the course of their work, the Commissioners discovered not only the exploitation of children but also brought to light the employment of adult females at the coal face and immediately extended their brief to include them. Their evidence outlined, with strong moral overtones, the unsuitability of this work for women, often stressing examples of pits where due to extreme heat women worked stripped to the waist. As a result, Parliament passed the Coalmines Regulation Act in 1842 which excluded all female labour from working underground. Nevertheless, the girls remained at the pit brow sorting and transporting coal.

Munby's first visit to Wigan was in 1853 but of this we have no information as his diaries do not begin until six years later. In total he visited Wigan on seventeen occasions and for the last time in 1887. We can only speculate on why he was so interested in Wigan pit girls, but one possible explanation is that there was a greater concentration of pit girls working in the Wigan area than anywhere else in the country. Due to the fact that census returns in the 19th century were often incomplete and that many women worked at collieries for only short periods, it is difficult to estimate just how many Wigan pit girls there were in employment at any one time. According to the 1861 census there were over 9,000 coalminers in Wigan compared with only 281 pit women. The census also shows that the main employment for women was in the mills which accounted for almost 90% of the female workforce in the town. But by the mid 1880s the number of Wigan pit girls had grown to an estimated seven to eight hundred compared with a national figure of 4,500 girls working on the surface at coal mines. The pit girls in Wigan were a minority but they were a sizeable enough minority to attract Munby's interest.

There was also one unique feature of the women who worked in the Wigan coalfield: they wore trousers, and this attracted a lot of attention. Munby, ever eager to investigate minute details of their lives, discovered that trousers were worn by pit women within a ten mile radius of the town. The women had worn trousers when employed underground and had continued to wear them when working on the surface. By the mid 1860s Ince Hall Pits, which were close to the town centre, had to ban all visitors to the pit brow as people gathered to see the girls wearing trousers.

A House of Commons Select Committee set up in 1865 to consider the continued employment of women at the pit brow heard evidence concerning the pit girls "peculiarity of dress". Strong attacks were made in the national press against the coal districts that employed women at the pit brow who were dressed in male attire and whose work was considered by many, particularly men, to be unsuitable for females.

Possibly to counteract these accusations, Ince Hall Pits sent all their pit girls in early 1866 to be photographed by Wigan professional photographer John Cooper. The picture were submitted as evidence to the Select Committee, and these of Sarah and Ellen Fairhurst in their Sunday cloths (photographs nos.49, 50) may have been part of that evidence. Cooper appears to have stressed the femininity of the girls by posing them against attractive backdrops. In contrast, his photographs of Ann Fairhurst and Jane Brown in their working clothes (nos. 54, 55) were shot in deliberately stark surroundings. The photographs presented by Ince Hall Pits played a part in convincing the Select Committee that there was little difference between the work of the pit girls and the work done by women in other manual jobs. The attempt to exclude women from mining altogether ground temporarily to a halt.

By the early 1860s Munby was able to supplement his diary entries by purchasing carte de visite portraits of pit girls by Wigan photographers Robert Little and Thomas Dugdale. Portraits of Wigan pit girls were also displayed outside their studios and sold very well. Munby not only bought these but also persuaded some of the women to be photographed specially for him. He knew a number of the girls well, seeing them on each visit to the town and establishing relationships that lasted some twenty to thirty years. It would be interesting to know what they thought of him. They appear to have viewed him as a slightly eccentric but friendly character, nicknaming him Th'inspector, and he would have particularly endeared himself through his readiness to distribute money among them.

Many of the photographs Munby bought were of girls in their late teens or early twenties. Most of the girls he met whose ages he noted were under twenty, although there were some women working at the pits at fifty years of age. In the main the pit girls were young adults living at home with their parents. Interestingly, very few of the girls he knew remained at the same pit between 1860 and the mid 1880's. There was considerable mobility for a variety of reasons. Some pits became exhausted and some of the girls who returned to mine work after having a baby went to work at a different colliery. Some changed jobs for more money.

In the mid 1860's the pit girls were employed "riddling" or sieving coal- using the large sieves they often carried in studio portraits- and shovelling coal into wagons or barges. Gradually, with more pit owners installing screens, the main job of the women was to sort coal at the picking belts. Screens were introduced to separate different sizes of coal by placing fixed bars at a set distance from each other.

The women's job was to stand at the belts inspecting the coal and removing all dirt by hand. The pit girls worked hard and at a furious pace. A description by Munby of Douglas Bank Colliery in 1878 provides an example: "girls thrutching (pushing) full corves (baskets) from the pit shaft or kicking them over at the screens, girls with their spades standing in the holds of barges, girls standing in the railway trucks under the belts, arranging coal with their hands as each load came thundering down, girls climbing ladders and swinging to and fro from one level to another, and crouching and crawling in the coal shoots, hid in the clouds of black dust".

A new Mines Bill introduced by the Liberal government in the 1880's provided another opportunity for those opposed to women working in mining. Still outside the union and with many miners seeing women as cheap labour or as taking men's jobs, the women were in danger of being isolated. But a local campaign was launched led by the Reverend Harry Mitchell, the vicar of St. John's, Pemberton and the Mayoress of Wigan, Margaret Park, to defend the pit girls' right to work. A deputation of girls from Wigan went to London to see the Home Secretary to explain their position. The threat to the women's jobs was averted but another deputation of pit women had to visit Parliament in 1911 when the issue was raised again.

Gradually, the mechanisation of many surface jobs and the closure of pits reduced the number of women working in mining. During the First World War the number of pit girls actually increased but the end came in the 1950's. The National Coal Board and the National Union of Mineworkers agreed that disabled miners should have preference over women for surface jobs. Often women were offered alternative employment cleaning or working in canteens. By the late 1960's there were no pit brow lasses working anywhere in the Lancashire coalfield.

For more information on Wigan's pit brow women, the following books are essential reading:
Michael Hiley: Victorian working women: portraits from life. Gordon Frase 1979.
Angela V. John: By the sweat of their brow: women workers in Victorian coal mines. Croom Helm 1980.

49,50. Sarah and Ellen Fairhurst in their Sunday clothes. Women had been excluded from working underground in 1842. In 1865 a House of Commons Select Committee was set up to consider the continued employment of women at the pit head. Much attention focused on the Wigan pit girls wearing trousers, a form of dress certain to outrage Victorian ideas of decency and femininity. Possibly to diffuse this explosive issue, Ince Hall Pits sent all their broo wenches in early 1866 to be photographed by John Cooper in his Wigan studio and submitted the portraits to the Select Committee as evidence. These photographs may have been included though Munby dates Sarah's portrait as 1867 when she was 19. Her sister Ellen was a slack washer at Bottomplace Pit. By the mid 1870's there was as increasing demand for small coal used in coke making. At Ince Hall Ellen and another pit lass cleaned the small coal by raking it in a large trough as it was carried along by a stream of water. This work was highly prized as it was undercover and paid more- as much as two shillings a week.

44

51

52

51. Ellen Grounds, filler of Rose Bridge Pits. This carte de visite by Robert Little, one of the earliest recorded photographers in Wigan, was taken in 1866 when Ellen was 17.

52. Ellen Grounds in her Sunday best, 1866 Carte de visite by Robert Little.

53. Ellen Grounds and A.J. Munby. When this photograph was taken by Robert Little on 11th September 1873 Ellen was 22 and was working at Pearson & Knowles' Arley mine. She had started work as a pit girl at the age of 13 and had previously worked as a factory girl and a maid of all work. Munby, often obsessed by the physical size of the "broo wenches", stood beside her "to show how nearly she approached me in size".

54. Ann Fairhurst, Ince Hall Pits. A carte de visite taken by John Cooper in 1868.

55. Jane Brown of Bottomplace Pit. Carte de visite by John Cooper.

56. This photograph of Jane Brown by John Cooper was possibly taken in 1866 when Jane was 22. In that year Ince Hall Pits sent all their pit girls to Cooper's studio to be photographed. She had earlier worker at Rose Bridge Pits and came from a family of colliers. By the mid 1880's, Jane was married and had left work but her daughter Mary was a pit girl working at Alexandra Pit, Whelley.

55

56

47

57. Welsh Nan (Mary Ann Morgan) photographed by Robert Little in 1867. Mary had worked at the mines in Merthyr but when her parents died she left colliery work and went into service in Birkenhead. She later returned to pit work when she moved to Hindley. Most of the pit girls were daughters living at home but some like Welsh Nan were lodgers. She shared with several mill girls and paid a weekly rent of 1s 3p.

58. Mr. Wright, landlord of the Three Crowns, 16 Standishgate and two pit wenches. The girls worked at the Mains colliery in Bryn owned by Cross, Tetley and Co. Ltd. Munby bought this photograph in March 1865. It was taken by Louisa (Lucy) Millard, a member of the famous Millard family of Wigan photographers.

59. Alice Heywood in 1887. A less formal photograph than the studio portraits of her cousin, Jane Brown. Alice worked at Alexandra Pit Whelley. First sunk in 1873, the pit's name commemorated the visit of the Prince of Wales and Princess Alexandra to Haigh Hall in that year.

60. Thomas Dugdale appeared to understand Munby's interest in working women and supplied him with the type of photographs he required. These superb photographs come from a series of studies of pit brow women he took at collieries in the Shevington area in the mid 1860's.

61. & 62. For quite some time Munby had been trying to persuade Thomas Dugdale to produce some location pictures for him, and these three images (nos 60,61 and 62) are amongst the earliest examples of location portraits in Munby's collection.

They are interesting in more than the normal historical respect of the subject matter. The portrait photographer of the 1850s and early 1860s had a major drawback to overcome before embarking on location photography. These were the days before mass production of photographic plates, and the photographer had to make his own. The "wet collodion" process gave excellent results but the plates had to be prepared and coated immediately before use, exposed before before the collodion dried, and developed straight afterwards. This meant that the location photographer had to take a portable darkroom with him wherever he went.

62

By the early 1860s, however, several Manchester photographers and chemists were working on a dry version of the process - amongst them J.T. Chapman, James Mudd and Joseph Sidebotham. The dry plate had the one major advantage that it could be prepared days before use - and was in fact the first step towards mass produced materials which we we enjoy today. It had the great disadvantage that it was many times less sensitive than the wet version - requiring long exposures even in relatively bright sunshine. These three pictures are taken between 1864 and 1867 and it may well be that with them Dugdale was experimenting with just such a dry plate. The need for long exposure could account for the unusually 'posed' look of the girls, and the fact that they are all photographed resting firmly against something solid. Compare these rather rigid portraits with the studio portraits by Cooper, Millard and others earlier in this chapter - there the poses are much more natural thanks to the shorter exposures the wet plate process permitted in the studio.

53

63. A Daguerreotype, photographer unknown, taken about 1850. This process, introduced in 1839 produced a direct positive image on a polished silvered copper plate. Daguerreotypes are easily recognisable due to the high level of reflection from their surface - at some viewing angles the picture appears positive, while at others it appears negative. It is unlikely that any resident Wigan photographer used this process, although travelling photographers may have used it while visiting the town.

64. The Collodion Positive, or Ambrotype process produced a direct positive on glass. There was no negative, and further copies could only be made either at the time of the original sitting, or by copying another ambrotype. This process was highly popular between 1851 and the late 1860s. Wigan photographers such as Craig, Platt and Little would almost certainly have used this process. The picture were supplied in small leather covered and velvet lined cases to protect then from damage and excess light. Some photographers had their names and addresses gold blocked on to the back of the case while others simply slipped a business card into the case under the photograph. Others did neither leaving us none the wiser as to who they were. No ambrotypes bearing the names of Wigan photographers have yet been discovered.

Professional Photography in Wigan

Photography, in a practical commercial form, dates from about 1840. The first photographs were taken in the late 1820s, but the processess used were to slow to allow the commercial expoitation of the new medium. It was not until the work of a Frenchman, Louis Daguerre, and an Englishman, Henry Fox Talbot in the late 1830s that practical and potentially commercial photographic processes started to appear.

The first process to be used professionally was the French Daguerreotype process, launched in 1839, and in use in photographic portrait studios throughout the country from the early 1840s.

Manchester's first studio opened in Ducie Place in 1841 - so it is likely that a town the size of Wigan would have at least been visited regularly by a photographer within about two years - late 1842 or early 1843.

Surprisingly, however, despite rigorous searching, we have not yet come up with a name or a date to support that proposition. Other towns in the area and similar in size and distance from Manchester had at least one studio by the mid 1840s but Wigan, for some reason was either very late in getting in on the act - or kept particularly quiet about it.

The Daguerreotype was immensely popular as a medium for portraiture, but represented a false start in photography. The picture was produced on a silvered copper plate giving a direct positive image - there was no negative. It was a very detailed image, but very fragile and easily damaged. For that reason the pictures were kept in small velvet lined cases - already widely available as the standard packaging for miniature paintings - often decorated with elaborate patterns and motifs on the outer faces.

These same cases were used from the early 1850s for the Ambrotype, or collodion positive, another direct positive photographic process this time using a glass plate instead of the silvered copper plate of the Daguerreotype. Ambrotypes were a lot cheaper than Daguerreotypes, but still too expensive to be within the budget of the majority of people.

The Ambrotype was a variation on the wet collodion process introduced in 1851 by Frederick Scott Archer. Wet collodion could be used to produce either the ambrotype positive, or a glass plate negative from which any number of prints could be made. That ease of duplication brought prices down and when, in the late 1850s the small carte de visite print was introduced - bringing prices within just about everybody's reach - portrait photography for the masses really became a reality and the numbers of photographers multiplied several-fold almost overnight.

Prices were as low as half a crown for the actual photographic session and a dozen prints, although photographers had a sliding scale of charges according to the pose, setting and the quality of finish they gave to their work. James Millard charged as little as one shilling for taking the photograph and producing three prints. For three shillings, twelve prints were available - usually from four slightly different negatives as the cameras used took four pictures on a single plate. One plate (four poses) printed three times gave the twelve prints. The lowest prices brought no frills whatsoever to the photographic session - a simple portrait against a plain background. For sixpence more for three, or five shillings a dozen, the portrait would be taken against a painted background - a garden scene, a lavish room interior or balcony scene - and printed on a slightly glossier type of paper. For the most expensive cartes, James Millard would introduce a wooden balustrade, or fine-looking furniture or some other trappings of affluence into the setting and charge seven shillings a dozen for the resulting prints.

The carte de visite also introduced a whole range of stationary to the photographic market - from the cards themselves on to which the prints were pasted, to the lavishly decorated family albums which became an essential feature of most Victorian drawing rooms. The best cards and the best albums were produced in France, by Marion & Co. of Paris, and it was from Marion's that Millard bought his first blank cards when he opened his first studio in Millgate. London printers were used for a second version of the card a few years later when his second studio at Scholes Bridge was opened, but he returned to Marion for the ornate cream and red cards which became the hallmark of Millard photographs in the late 1870s and 80s when his Market Street studios were at their height. Towards the end of the Market Street studio's existance, gold lettering on dark green cards, again produced in France, were used. The same type of card was used by Herbert Wragg for his 45 Mesnes Street studio up to the end of the nineteenth century. The backs and fronts of Victorian cartes de visite are themselves an interesting reflection of changing tastes, becoming simpler as the century drew to a close.

With the carte de visite - so named because it was the traditional size of the Victorian visiting card - photography's major collecting craze was introduced, and soon family albums throughout the country contained, in addition to family and friends, photographs of the famous and infamous of the day - royalty, religious and political leaders, oddities such as dwarfs, Siamese twins and so on. Most local photographers increased their turnover selling the work of the large London studios - the London Photographic & Stereoscopic Company had several thousand 'stock' photographs which they sold wholesale to almost every local photographer in the country. A single carte de visite of Queen Victoria could be bought for a few pence, making the photographic album into much more than just a book full of memories. It became in many ways a reference book of what people looked like, giving people in towns like Wigan a chance to see what the Queen, the Prime Minister, the leading musicians and artists all looked like. At a time when newspapers could not carry photographs, and there were none of todays means of letting the nation see what its leaders looked like, this aspect of the photographic trade served a very useful purpose indeed.

Our research has allowed us to compile a list of over eighty photographers working in Wigan before the end of the First World War. The earliest dated reference of a photographic studio in the town's trade directories is 1853 - some ten or more years after the first photographic studios opened in Manchester and Liverpool.

There are a number of possible reasons why it should have taken so long for Wigan to get its first permanent professional photographer. Firstly, there is the undoubted fact that Wigan was never a rich town - the social and financial structure of the town was such that until photography became truly inexpensive, few people could have afforded to meet the prices charged for professional portraiture. Wigan, like many of the Northern industrial towns did not have a resident artist in the 1840s (that being the traditional way of getting a portrait) so it is hardly surprising that it was slow to acquire a photographer. Indeed only the popular seaside resorts of Blackpool and Southport sported their own photographic studios before 1853. In the 1840s professional photographers needed a license to work, as the process used at the time, the Daguerreotype, was covered by strictly enforced patents. When the Ambrotype process was introduced in 1851 there was no need for a license, but few photographers who were not already established entered the market place at that time. Both processess existed side by side for some years and photographers offering one invariably also offered the others. As the licence fee were high, the photographers picked their towns with great care to make sure that there was a reasonable return on their outlay. The pickings in Wigan would not have been very rich.

The introduction of photography into the town would therefore have been left to travelling photographers

-perhaps from a Manchester or Liverpool studio - setting up temporary studios in boarding houses or pubs and offering their services for a few weeks before moving on.

Wigan's first three resident photographers were Charles Craig at 16 King Street, Robert Little of Clarence Yard, and James Platt of 32 Church Street. Little is known of Charles Craig - and none of his pictures have yet turned up, but Robert Little is rather better known - as was his wife who probably had more to do with the successful operation of the studio than her husband did. Platt seems to have been uncertain that photography could support him exclusively, for he advertised himself as photographer and insurance agent - operating an agency for the Liverpool London & Globe Insurance Company.

James Platt was not alone in keeping more than one string to his bow - several others kept a second source of income to help out during photography's lean times. In doing so, they were continuing a tradition which had started with the travelling photographers - for several of Wigan's photographers in the 1860s were also landlords of town centre public houses. In addition to offering a second source of income, the idea of a publican who was also a photographer may have had a sound business basis - as several travelling photographers had already established the idea of a photographic studio in an upstairs room at the 'local'.

John Cooper a beer retailer since the early 1860s had been operating a studio for about three years at 15 Harrogate Street, before he took over as landlord of the Royal Oak in Standishgate in 1866, taking his photographic business with him. Indeed he maintained the dual role of photographer and publican for over thirty years, moving first to the Green Man Inn in Standishgate complete with his cameras in the early 1870s, and then to the Harrogate Inn in Harrogate Street. In taking over the Green Man, he was exchanging one pub with a photographic studio for another pub with a photographic studio - for Thomas George Dugdale, the previous landlord of the Green Man had also established a studio in 1863 at the very latest. Dugdale moved his studio to Upholland before 1872.

Mrs. Cooper appears to have worked alongside her husband in both bar and studio at the Harrogate Inn - and probably the two previous pubs as well - until the mid 1890s when John Cooper moved to an exclusively photographic business in Poolstock, leaving his wife to operate both the pub and the portrait studio on her own. This may have been in order to separate two branches of their photographic business which had been developed side by side over a period of years - while Mrs. Cooper became an established portrait photographer producing cartes de visite at the lower end of the price ladder, her husband became a very accomplished architectural photographer, and was regularly commissioned by the civic authorities to produce architectural records for them of the changing face of the town.

When James Millard opened his first photographic

65. & 66. Two aspects of the work of John Cooper's studio. The portrait bears the Royal Oak address on the reverse and may have been taken either by John Cooper or his wife. The view of Church gates probably dates from either Green Man studio, or Cooper's later Poolstock studio.

67. Officers of the Wigan territorials, outside the Drill Hall, taken by F. Dew about 1917.

68. Charles Laws had a studio in Wallgate near North Western Station.

studio in the early 1870s, he was already well known in the town. His first entry in a local trade directory in 1869 lists him as a hardware dealer, but three years later in 1872 he is listed as Photographer, Hardware Dealer, Auctioneer, Valuer, Optician and Picture Framer! His first studio was at 118 Millgate with a second opened at Scholes Bridge by the mid 70s. In the 1880s he closed the Millgate studio and moved to Market Street "opposite the new Market Hall" and traded from a number of Market Street addresses well into this century. A studio in Makinson Arcade opened early in this century was run by his two sons, who at one time had also had a professional portrait studio in Needles California.

James Millard's sister - Lucy or Louisa (she used both names) had been operating a portrait studio in Hope Street for some many years before James entered the business. In the 1860s and early 1870s, first as Lucy Millard and later under her married name of Mawson, she produced portraits in a small studio which was demolished at the turn of century to make way for the building which later became Morrisons Supermarket and has itself now been demolished to make way for the Galleries. She seems to have given up photography - in Wigan at least - by the mid 1870s and moved to Southport.

Professional photography enjoyed its greatest popularity as far as portraiture was concerned in the 1890s and early 1900s. Wigan was no exception in this respect and more of our total list of photographers were working in this period than at any other time. We have located only three studios from the 1850s, increasing to ten for the 1860s. By the 1870s the number had increased to a dozen with fourteen, ten years later. By the 1890s the number was at least twenty, with probably several more for whom we cannot get precise dates. At the beginning of the Great War there are again about twenty - although not the same twenty as before - and by 1920, the final date of our survey, only seven or eight. In the town today there are two. Although both of them concentrate on wedding photography - unheard of in the Victorian period - they do produce a small amount of portraiture. It was portraiture which was the mainstay of our eighty and more photographers and which kept them in business. The idea of going to a professional photographer for an informal portrait started to die out with the introduction of the Kodak Brownie camera in the 1890s and with simple and cheap cameras available by the outbreak of War, portraiture never really recovered. The majority of people now only use a professional portrait photographer for the most formal of occasions.

The popular locations for photographic studios in Wigan were Standishgate, Wallgate and Mesnes Street. At varying times, Standishgate had photographic studios at Nos 21, 22a, 30, 38, 48, 70, 78, 96, 104, 111, and 130. In the mid 1880s there was even a time when six of them were open at the same time - Brown Barnes & Bell at No30, John Cooper at the Royal Oak No111, Harrison at No38, Hill at No48, A & G Taylor at No78, and Allen & Co. who declined to put the number of their building in the 1887 trades directory.

Four of the addresses were pubs. A & G Taylor had their studio in the Griffin, Hill in the Rose, Cooper in the Royal Oak and Thomas Dugdale and later John Cooper in the Green Man.

In Mesnes Street the most popular address for a photographic studio was No45 - now part of Smiths Bookshop who published this book. It was from this address that Herbert Wragg worked from about 1880, first on his own and then as Wragg & Co. with his son. The premises were still in use as a photographic studio well into the 1920s operated by Turner Brothers & Raymond.

While the majority of our listed photographers worked exclusively in portraiture, a few did leave their marks on other branches of photography. John Cooper's architectural work has already been mentioned. To that can be added fine architectural views of local collieries - Bamfurlong in particular - by Thomas Taylor of Platt Bridge, and some excellent architectural work by James Millard. Millard also advertised himself as a landscape photographer although so far no examples of this aspect of work have come to light. He was also an optician and instrument maker - particularly well known for his design and manufacture of telescopes, combining an abiding hobby with his business acumen. A Rudolph Douglas also produced records of Wigan's buildings for the Borough records.

Records of civic events such as the visits of King George V, were photographed by Harry Lathom of Park Cresent. Cooper was on hand to photograph the visit to Wigan by the philanthropist Andrew Carnegie, and it was to Harry Parkes that the task fell of producing the first pictures of the devastation in the aftermath of the Maypole Colliery explosion in 1908.

In all a rich photographic heritage which is still being rediscovered. The work of these, and perhaps other as yet unrecognised Wigan photographers, may fill future volumes of these books.

The listings which follow give approximate dates for the working lives of professional photographers in Wigan between 1853 and 1920. In many cases the dates can be taken as accurate only to plus or minus two years, the frequency of the trade directories from which much of the information has been gleaned. Other dates have been added from searches of dated pictures in the archives of Wigan Metro at Leigh and from the files of the Wigan Observer, as well as from dated information provided by friends and associates.

The list is not likely to be complete as there may very well have been studios the lifetime of which fell unfortunately between the publication of one trade directory and the compilation of the next.

Allen & Co. Standishgate,	1887
American Photo Co (the) 45 Mesnes Street	1931
Arthur Fred, Ltd, 45 Mesnes Street	1918
Ashurst, Arthur 274 Ormskirk Rd.	1910-19
Ashurst & Meadows, 290(back)Ormskirk Rd. Pemberton	1909-1910
Baldwin Thomas Joseph 92 Great George Street	1865
Baron James Corporation Street Poolstock	1869
Barton John Worsley Mesnes, Photographer & Confectioner	1869
Benson Station Road	1880-1885
Bent Mrs. Elizabeth P 28 Frog Lane	1891-1898
Berry, Harry Station Road	1913
Bibby Robert, Photographer & Confectioner Water Heyes	1869
Blackburn James, 5 Birch Street	1903-1918
60 Scot Lane	1920
Brazendale, James, 71 Mesnes Street	1903
24 Mesnes Street	1905
45 Darlington Street	1909-1910
Brittania Electric Portraits Ltd, 22a Standishgate	1920
Brown Barnes & Bell 30 Standishgate	1881-1885
Buckley Thomas C, 48 Standishgate	1920
Cooper, Mrs. Alice, 7 Harrogate Street	1895-1898
Cooper, John, 15 Harrogate Street	1863-1865
Royal Oak Hotel, 111 Standishgate	1866-1869
Green Man Inn, Standishgate	1881-1885
Harrogate Inn, Harrogate Street	1886-1890
30 Poolstock	1903

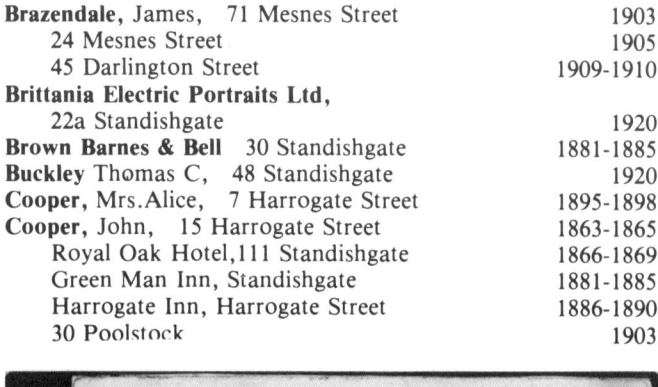

69. The ornate back of one of Laws' carte de visite photographs about 1882.

70. Robert Little went for a simpler motif on the back of his cartes.

73. James Millard outside his Market Street studio at the turn of the century. He designed and built the studio himself, on the site now occupied by the Queen's Hall. The photograph was taken by one of his sons.

71. James Millard had several studios in the town over a period of years. His involvement with professional photography spanned several changes in Victorian stlye and flambouyancy and these are all reflected in the designs of the backs of his cartes de visite. The earliest cartes list 118 Millgate only, then the Scholes studio is added. The Market Street studio then replaced the Millgate one,

72a 72b 72c. The fronts of cartes, 71a, 71b, and 71c, 1870s.

Craig Charles, 16 King Street	1853-1861
Crippen, E.R. 2 Spring Bank, Pemberton	1895
Oak Lea, Billinge Road Pemberton	1898
Crippen & Co, 2 Spring Bank Pemberton	1903
Market Square, Wigan	1904-1910
Derbyshire, Pemberton	1920
Dew, Fred W, 1 Parsons Walk	1913-1920
Douglas, A.Rudolph, 23 Upper Dicconson Street	1889-1905
Dugdale Thomas George,	
Green Man Inn, Standishgate	1863-1869
& 21 Standishgate	1869
Up Holland	from 1872
Foley Cyril, 96 Standishgate	1913-1920
Hall James, 96 Standishgate	1909-1910
Harrison Brothers, 38 Standishgate	1885
Heaton, Alfred E, Colin Street	1905
4 Douglas Road (& Insurance Agent)	1909-1913
Hill, Joseph, 48 Standishgate	1898-1900
Hill, William, 48 Standishgate	1903
Hill & Son, 48 Standishgate	1905-1910
Holliday & Major, 7 Ryland Street	1898
Holliday, William, 7 Ryland Street	1901
Hurst, William, Clapgate Lane, Goose Green.	1905-1920
Jones David, 67 Worsley Mesnes	1881
Lathom Herbert 1 Park Cresent & 15 Park Road	1910-1920
Laws, Charles H. Wallgate	1881-1882
Leslie Brothers, 22 Hope Street	1918
Leyland, James, Park Lane, Abram	1898-1901
Little Robert 2, Clarence Yard	1853-1885
Lowe, Charles, Station Road	1918
Marsh, Thomas, 812 Ormskirk Road	1905
685 Ormskirk Road	1920
Mawsom, Lucy 4 Hope Street (see Millard Lucy)	1872
Millard, James, 118 Millgate	1872
118 Millgate & Scholes Bridge	1875
19 Market Street & Scholes Bridge	1881-1898
Market Street	1891
Market Street & 1 Douglas Road	1891-1892
Millard & Company, 70 Market Street	1903-1920
Makinson Arcade	1920s
Millard, Lucy 4 Hope Street	1865-1872
Nicholson, George, 17 Birkett Bank	1887-1888
O'Reilly, Gregory, 47, Darlington Street	1898

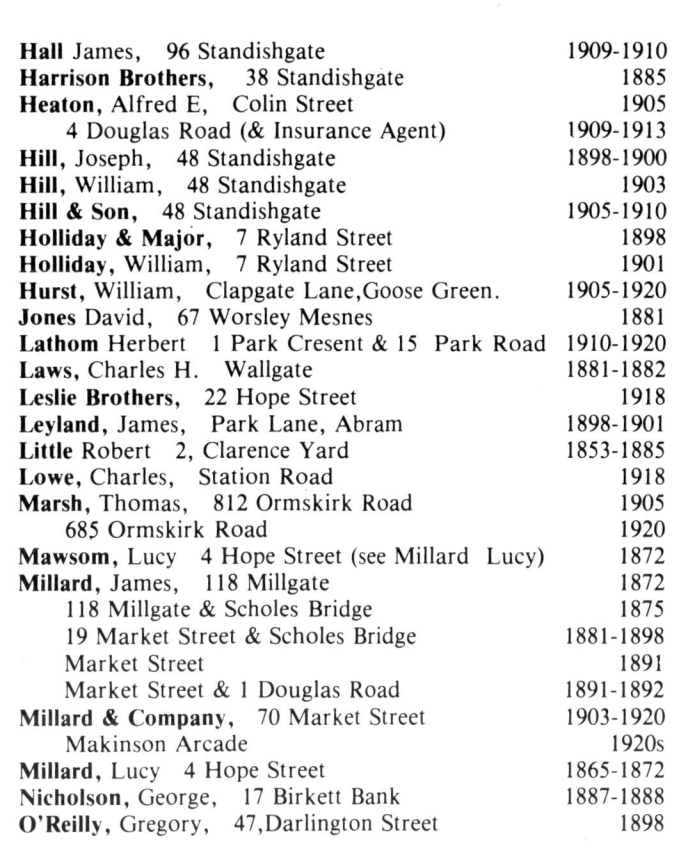

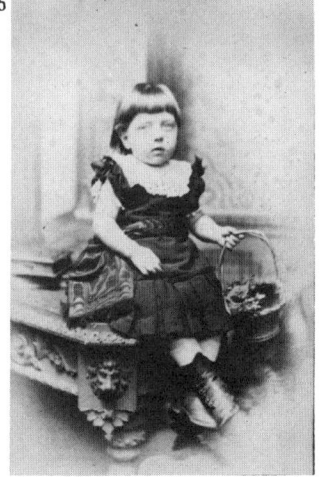

74. Harry Parkes was one of the first local newspaper photographers. This study of coal pickers was published in March 1912 during the great coal strike.

75. Thomas Taylor of Platt Bridge produced a series of views of local collieries and colliery workers in the first few years of the 1900s. This is Bamfurlong Colliery.

76. This portrait, taken by Herbert Wragg about 1900 in a studio which occupied the site of what is now the left hand window of Smiths Bookshop.

Parkes, Harry, 14, Smiths Road, Orrell	1900-1910	**Taylor,** Andrew & George, 25b King St.	1811-1882
Parsons, H. 7 Darlington Street	1920	78 Standishgate	1890
Pemberton Photographic Company,		Moot Hall Chambers, 2 Wallgate	1903-1905
15 Spring Bank,	1903	**Taylor Brothers,** 1 New Square	1910
(see Sedgewick) 15 Billinge Road	1905	48 Standishgate	1909-1913
Platt, James,		**Taylor,** Thomas, Platt Bridge	1898-1901
Photographer & Insurance Agent,		**Tinsley,** E.A. & Co, 78 Standishgate	1890
32 Church Street	1853-1861	**Van Esty & Company,** 48 Standishgate	1913
Pollard, Graham, 22 Market Square&Hope Street	1909-1910	**Vitali,** Emanuele, 41 Wallgate	1890
Potts, Hartley & Nicholson Birkett Bank (see		**Wallace,** William, 72 Preston Rd. Standish	1901
Nicholson)	1890-1905	**Welton,** Joseph E. 104 Standishgate	1909-1913
Rattray, James, 38 Standishgate	1891	**Wigan Photographic Studio,** the,	
Rattray, John S. 232 Wallgate	1909-1910	38 Standishgate	1895
Richardson & Scott, Station Road	1905	**Williams,** John, 70 Standishgate	1891
Roberts, Tinsley & Co. no address found	1885	**Wild,** Issac, Wallgate	1881
Sedgewick, John, 15 Billinge Road, Pemberton	1909-1910	**Williams,** S. Clarence Chambers, Wallgate	1903
Sedgewick, Mrs. E. 104 Standishgate	1918	**Worswick,** Joseph, Tower Buildings, Wallgate	1913-1918
Skewes, William, 1 Park Cresent	1905-1910	**Wragg,** Herbert, 45 Mesnes Street	1885-1910
Smith, no address found (estimate)	1910	**Wragg & Son,** 45 Mesnes Street	1898
Stevenson, Vincent, 203 Warrington Road, Abram	1905	**Wright,** William, Marsh Lane	1869
Stringler, L. 48 Standishgate	1918	5 St. George's Street	1872
Sylvester & Doran, 70 Standishgate	c1920	Marsh Street	1876
Turner Brothers & Raymond, 45 Mesnes Street	c1920		

77

77. A Cabinet Print from the Wragg & Sons studio also about 1900. The cabinet print was introduced in the 1860s for those customers who found the carte de visite altogether too small. It gave a print size about three times the size of the carte - about 10cm x 15cm as opposed to the carte de visite which measured only 9cm x 5½cm unmounted on a 10½cm x 6½cm card.

78. Carte de visite by Thomas Dugdale, taken at his studio in the Green Man Inn about 1863 for Arthur Munby.

79. Stereoscopic photograph by S. S. Lees of St. Helens, 1865. The Pit Brow Girls worked at Rose Bridge Colliery, owned by John Morris. Surprisingly, in view of the popularity of the stereoscopic view - which gave a three-dimensional image when viewed through a special viewer - this is the only stereoscopic photograph from the Wigan coalfield which has so far come to light. At the height of the stereo craze in the mid to late 1860s a viewer and a selection of cards could be found in all but poorest Victorian drawing rooms. The principle involved taking two photographs simultaneously with a twin lens camera, the lenses the same distance apart as the human eyes. When the prints were viewed through a specially designed viewer - the left eye looking at the left hand picture and the right eye looking at the right hand one - a full three dimensional image with all the depth and perspective of the original scene was recreated. The cards cost about half a crown (12½p) for three and were sold widely through photographic studios and local bookshops and newsagents.